THE
Unspoken
Dialogue

*Understanding Body Language and
Controlling Interviews and Negotiations*

SECOND EDITION

What People Are Saying...

A very useful tool to understand non-verbal language . . .
>*Norbert Reiss*
>Germany

Robert Rail is consummate in conveying the meaning of a universally recognized basic language - *body language* - which few, if any, give any thought to at any given time . . .
>*Ruma Bhattacharji*
>India

This book is so instructive that wherever you are in the world you can pick it up and start instructing. It is applicable in any language or culture. A multi-lingual masterpiece!
>*Per Ersgard*
>Sweden

This material is a result of his hard work in the service for peace . . . mastery in body signs.
>*Evgueni Olmeltchenko*
>Russia

This is obviously the culmination of great experience and knowledge . . . As a lecturer he was as outstanding as the book.
>*Ali Abdel Halim*
>Jordan

Bob's knowledge of human behavior and his experience as a police officer combine to formulate "Body Signs" . . . it has been enjoyed and understood around the world.
>*Graham Ridding*
>ITSS - United Nations

It was magnificent . . . Outstanding topic of great need! . . .

Francois Vigneron
France

After having been with the Danish Police Force for over twenty years I still learned a lot from Mr. Rail's teaching!

Steen Fleusborg
Denmark

There is always the hue and cry from political aspirants about minimum force . . . In the end, the Law Enforcement officers and their employers become liable victims. Thanks to Bob Rail, employer's financial liability levels will be greatly reduced. It would be wise for agencies to include the techniques in this book in their training package.

Augustine Sewoatsri
Ghana

THE
Unspoken
Dialogue

*Understanding Body Language and
Controlling Interviews and Negotiations*

SECOND EDITION

Robert R. Rail, Ph.D.

VARRO PRESS

The *Unspoken* Dialogue
Understanding Body Language and Controlling Interviews and Negotiations

SECOND EDITION

Robert R. Rail, Ph.D.

VARRO PRESS
P.O. Box 8413
Shawnee Mission, Kansas 66208 USA
Tel: 913-385-2034
Web: www.varropress.com

Copyright © 2009 Robert R. Rail

All rights reserved. No part of this book may be reprinted or reproduced or utilized in any form or by electronic, mechanical or other means now known or hereafter invented, including photocopying and recording, or in any information storage or retrieval system, without the written permission of the publisher, Varro Press, Inc., except by a reviewer, who may quote brief passages in a review.

Publisher's Cataloging-In-Publication

Rail, Robert R.
 The unspoken dialogue : understanding body language and controlling interviews and negotiations / by Robert R. Rail. -- 2nd ed.
  p. cm.
  LCCN: 2005937316
  ISBN: 978-1-888644-17-3

 1. Body language. 2. Negotiation in business. 3. Employment interviewing. I. Title.

BF637.N66R35 2001   153.6'9
                  QBI00-500164

Printed and bound in the United States of America

Table of Contents

Foreword ix
Preface xi
Introduction xvii

PART ONE
BODY LANGUAGE

Understanding Body Language 20
    Definition of Terms 20
What The Body Is Saying 22
    The Eyes 22
    The Head 26
    The Arms 27
    The Hands 28
    The Feet 29
Examples of Body Language 32
Hand Gestures – *What The Hands Are Saying* 34
Extreme Circumstances 37

PART TWO
INTERACTIVE DIALOGUE

The Conversational Distance 40
The Volume Factor 44
Confrontational Positioning 45
Escalating Aggression 48
The Friendly Attack 51
Gestures – *The "Missing Link" To Understanding* 52

PART THREE
MANIPULATING DIALOGUE

Control – *Are You In Control?* 56
Changing Their Direction – *Keeping The Dialogue Flowing* 57
The Group – *Many As One* 59
The Agenda – *Better Yours Than Theirs* 60
The Other Team 60
Basic Personality Types You May Encounter 61
   The Enthusiastic Misdirector 61
      Body Language 62
      Solution 62
   The Quiet Ambusher 63
      Body Language 63
      Solution 64
   The Meeting Interviewer 64
      Body Language 65
      Solution 66
Dialogue To "The Authority" – *Who Do You Talk To?* 66
What Do They Really Want? – *Watching For The Subtle Signals* 67
The Gesture Mirror – *Using Natural Reactions* 69
Reacting To Displayed Gestures – *Your Quiet Control* 71
One On One – *Or One vs. One* 72
The Room – *A Conducive Environment* 74

SPECIAL THREAT SITUATIONS

Packages and Gestures 78
Apparel and Gestures 82

CONCLUSION

A Time For Advice 86

AFTERWORDS

Comments of William L. Budd 88
Comments of Jeffrey P. Rush 90
About the Author 93

FOREWORD

I met Bob Rail in Bosnia and attended a presentation he made about "body language." I was impressed. He cast some light on a series of problems which had been bugging me for a while. I was in Bosnia as a political officer for the UN. I had to deal with many difficult mediation and negotiation situations. I was an experienced field officer who had directed the activities of others, both in and after conflict.

What was bugging me was the "culture gap." The most obvious manifestation of which was the absolutely sincere dishonesty of all the parties I dealt with. None of them were completely dishonest all the time. They all had a fairly quickly identifiable party line of rhetoric. But consistently, they confused and tricked us. Simply put, we didn't understand them. We heard the words but couldn't read the whole message. One vital set of clues which could have helped us was "body language" - just to sort out what the real agenda items were - just to identify the real group leaders - just to reinforce our own message.

The more I learned about body language, the more I thought of my other experiences in the navy. I had eight years service in submarines. Today, the most sophisticated listening devices are used to detect and then analyze sounds in the ocean. By a combination of previous intelligence and comparing characteristics, the sounds of enemy submarines can be sorted out from many other sounds in the ocean - SOMETIMES!! One thing that any submarine hunter will tell you is "we get a lot of false alarms." You would be surprised at the number of sea creatures that can make noises identical to one part of a "submarine signature". What we always wanted was more information from another sensor to corroborate our acoustic data. Sometimes, if we were lucky, a patrolling aircraft using its radar would get a brief detection on something metallic that suddenly disappeared. We could correlate this information with our unconfirmed acoustic data and BINGO! - a submarine which had come up to the surface for a quick look was caught! Once we had this independent corroboration, life was so much easier.

It's the same with body language. A difficult negotiator is a "tough nut," which ever culture they come from. You need to gather all the clues. You need to pin your suspect down. Words are important, but rarely enough, even when you are operating in your own culture, let alone an alien one.

A big part of using all the signals is to adopt the attitude of what radio guys call "a wide ban scanner." Just relax and take in everything. Listen, Look, Sense and don't be too quick to jump to conclusions. Gradually, if you stay open to all the signals, the correct picture will present itself. You're listening carefully to what someone is saying; you're noticing all their movements, big and small; you're controlling yourself to not give off any hostile signals. Slowly, your senses, more than your purely rational mind, tell you, "this is a lie," or "they don't believe this themselves but have to say it." You have changed from purely receiving signals to analyzing and being able to take action.

Body language is not a brilliant, new revelation. Naturals have been doing it for centuries. All great communicators, both good and bad, have done it. If you look at film sequences of the great orators of the past, they used effective body language to control and direct their message. Using body language, both in reading others and reinforcing your own, will not, on its own, make you a millionaire. Body language is a super tool to use in all aspects of life to make you more effective, even if it only produces a small improvement. In many situations, the competitive edge will rely on this small margin. This is what fluency in body language can do for you.

If you are able to take in the common sense principles that are set out in this book, you will become a more effective communicator. You will be able to use these skills on both "offense" and "defense." Your personal relationship will benefit, you can consolidate work performance, and just feel more in control of your life.

Graham Day
Chief of Civil Affairs, United Nations, Sarajevo, Bosnia and Herzegovina

PREFACE

When did the idea for this book start? I really have no idea. It seems that I have always been a bit "verbally shy" expressing myself, and that will come as a total shock to most of my close friends, but I have! When I was very young, in school, I was always in the back of the room. Even to this day, as the person I have grown to be, I am still more comfortable in the back of the room or sitting with my back against the wall.

As a child I was always looking for that clue of how another child or adult was going to act toward me. Without even knowing what I was doing, I was reading their attitude toward me. By the time I reached the complexities of the fourth grade gulag of the Chicago school system I found myself doing better than most. Our daily internment was at the pleasure of "Mrs. Arthur" who displayed the body gestures of a drill sergeant. My classmates and I understood her body signs quite well. When she would pause while asking a question and look up at the ceiling, the next person to answer the question better get it correct. When she paced around the classroom, slapping her ruler into the palm of her hand to match the cadence of her footsteps, it was time to bury our noses in our books. We learned at a young age to watch out for our teacher's changing attitude.

Reflecting back on the twenty-four years I spent as a police officer, it was in itself, a never ending broad spectrum of body signs and behaviors that ran the gamut from ludicrous to blatantly obvious to remarkably professional. Among the most interesting of all of the circumstances associated with gesture displays was that of the interpersonal relationships in the rank and file. While most functioned with an excellent display of honor, dignity and bearing, there were those select few who greeted the higher ranks with all the self control of a puppy kept too long without being let out. At most of the department meetings and daily briefings I actually felt a little embarrassed for them as I watched them unknowingly display myriad of self disparaging gestures. They would sit as close as they could to the person in authority, and even move their chair closer if possible. They would maintain a consistent, agreeing nod while the person in authority was speaking. Their eyes would be wide open and looking at the person in authority. Their mouth would be slightly agape. They would be leaning forward in their chairs. The comments they would make would fall into the category of supportive grunts or a repeated "yes." They were totally subservient to authority. An interesting side light – when some of these individuals were promoted in rank (unfortunately), it

> The Unspoken Dialogue

was commonly noticed that the gestures displayed in the past toward that rank were no longer displayed to those who were now their contemporaries in status!

I don't remember how I ended up in Bosnia. I really don't! I vaguely remember reading something about American police being needed for teaching in war zones overseas. There was a deluge of never-ending physical training and testing and before I knew it I was on a plane over the ocean. As our plane was doing a routine, rapid decent landing in Sarajevo I remember looking out the window with my fellow American partners in this crazy quest and seeing devastation on the ground that I could not believe exists in our world today. There was no turning back now. I was proud to be an officer in the American contingent of the United Nations International Police Task Force.

There were three major groups in the war zone for us (the officers of 56 different countries) to contend with. There were the Serbs, the Croats, and the Bosnians. When they would be in a public area where they could meet, such as the "old market" place of Sarajevo, I would just sit quietly (with my back against the wall of course) in a little street side café and drink coffee (way too strong) and watch the show of body signs unveil before me. When members of the same group met, there was the usual, very close personal space between them. They would hug each other tightly. They would exchange kisses on the cheek and remain in physical contact throughout their brief hello. But in the Balkans, war has never laid down its ugly head and the hatred and pain remains as strong as it has for hundreds of years. When a person of one group meets a person of another group it seems as though the blood leaves their face and their eyes become ice. They see others as merely an image coming toward them. I was greeted with a small head nod and a narrow eye gaze. That was a very consistent gesture displayed by all three groups. Of course, the more the locals got to know me the more interactive they became with me.

When it came to interacting with my fellow international officers, it was a totally different situation. That is when I learned firsthand that the majority of communication is non-verbal. We wore the uniform of our own countries and the insignia of our task force. When we met, we always found a reason to eat, drink or just sit somewhere and take comfort in the safety of being more than one person. Many times I sat with a new friend from a country in Asia, Africa, Europe, or wherever else a plane can fly, and had coffee and a great time, not even knowing what we were saying to each other. Some things don't matter. We would sit close together with our eyes on the street and remark in our own language about what we saw - then just laugh or nod our heads in agreement about the world that surrounded us. To this day I still find it strangely remarkable that foreign mission colleagues can become so very close in such a short period of time. I have come to believe that the sharing of the most severe and threatening conditions and horrible incidents provides strength and friendship that words alone cannot describe.

After Bosnia I made what many would consider another calculated error in sane judgment. I was asked and was honored to go off to another war zone . . . Kosovo. I now found myself in Glogovach, Kosovo. It is located about 30 km from the capital city of Pristina, and is a bad mix of medieval border town and an AK-47 infested version of Tombstone, Arizona in the 1870's. If it weren't for the bad food there would be no food at all. Eating out of the plastic pouches gets old very quickly, and sharing your chow with dogs can be a problem when they become rabid the next time you run across them. You know that the air is bad when you brush your teeth and spit out a gritty paste and you didn't start with any tooth paste. The good news is that the violent situations kept our minds off of the bad conditions we were living in.

Thankfully, I was redeployed to the Pristina International Academy with the help of some old Bosnia buddies who needed me to teach with them, training the incoming international police. My new position was great. I was beyond thrilled and thankful to get out of Glogovach. My day at the academy would consist of teaching the officers of approximately fifty-nine countries about land mines, booby traps, use of force, and many other courses. Most of the social customs among the officers were different, as were their religions and languages. There were even situations where the language for the same country would have variations, and in some cases, the officers spoke in one language and wrote in another! It was a total mess of understanding but for me it was better than great! I could perceive one consistent factor between all of the different countries that transcended all of their differences. The body signs remained a constant between all the countries I trained! It was like I was given a tremendous gift of understanding that I could pass along.

In March of 2004, the worst thing that could happen did - the Kosovo riots! For the first forty-four hours, buildings with people still inside them, vehicles, and everything else that could burn was burned. For endless nights and smoke darkened days, we answered one call after another, drained of all emotion and body language. The gestures and responses slowly returned after the riots but for weeks, our reactions were abnormally extreme. We all laughed a little too loud at jokes, even the bad ones. Tempers were quick to flare up but fortunately, just as quick to burn out. We stayed more to ourselves than ever before. There was less eye contact and more of just a gaze through and past others. All of the other physical gestures were more muted. Hands were raised to ask a question, but not as high. We shook hands on meeting but would not reach out as far or squeeze as firmly. Friends would hug each other but then step back and look down. It is said that time heals all wounds, but the scars remain.

In Baghdad, Iraq, I had the privilege to spend over a year surrounded by an assortment of confrontation stress conditions and all the reactions that go with them. On some evenings, when the white hot sun went down, we would sit outside and just talk about back home and "getting out of this place." The stress level was high and the most stressed out colleagues talked the loudest. At times they even needed to be told to shut up and relax. (Under higher levels of stress people discuss very personal things in their lives that they would not normally talk about - but what is normal about a war zone!) We would be at a meeting or the chow hall when a rocket would fly over our heads and just sit there with a cup of coffee in our hands, watching the new guy fall out of his chair and run through a door whether it was open or not!

When I would be training the Shorta (Iraqi police) and a bomb blast would go off nearby I would joke about something else to get their minds (and mine) off of the conditions we were in. I could see the new, stress induced gestures the Shorta would display after the blast. They would sit up more erect in their chairs. They would fold their arms across their chest. They would pull their feet back underneath their chairs (Muslim etiquette frowns on crossing legs and displaying the bottoms of your feet). Their eyes would be open very wide and they would constantly look at the door of the room for a possible threat. Many of the Shorta would start tapping their fingers on their desk or exhibit other gesture habits as a stress outlet. When they would walk out of the training room on a break they would do one of three things: make a cell phone call to check on the safety of their family, light up a cigarette, or stand alone and just stare down at the ground. My conditioned reaction was to check my weapon and ammo, walk over to the main office and get a bottle of water, and then look from the classroom's second floor railing, over the city, to see where the smoke was coming from, to see how close the bomb blast was. This was my routine and I did it without even thinking.

Preface

When the Shorta left the training building at the end of the day they routinely took off their identification card and hid it in their pocket to avoid being detected as a police officer at a roadside check point so they would not be killed. When I saw the officers in my class start removing their ID's I knew they were eager to get home to their families.

Where did this book come from? I guess it has always been part of my life – We all have situational "non-verbal communication" every day. It is simply a matter of recognizing the body signs presented to us and knowing what they mean. I have learned a lot from the people I have met. Our verbal languages are as different as our backgrounds but the one constant is our body language. No matter where you come from in this world a smile is always a smile.

Robert R. Rail

INTRODUCTION

Regardless of where a person comes from or what verbal language they speak, they send a very clear message to us without ever uttering a word. The position of their body, and the placement and use of their arms, legs, head, and eyes all give us insight into this person beyond the conversation taking place in front of us. If we know how to interpret these messages from the body, it can greatly affect our ability to understand much more than the message of their words.

We all use signals from people who cannot speak, such as infants or persons who are ill or injured, and never give it a second thought. Too often, we forget about or ignore these signals when dealing with people who can speak. To fully understand what is taking place in front of us, we need to comprehend the total dialogue being presented, not just the spoken word.

As with any language, body language has many "dialects." The eyes, hands, and legs each have their own distinct nuances that are important at helping us understand what is being said. When you watch other people in conversation you can tell whether or not they are comfortable with each other. You have seen their body language and can "hear" what is not being said.

This book will help you recognize, understand, and evaluate the non-verbal messages of others. Part One: Body Language, explains the different gestures and mannerisms of body language. It will help you recognize the individual signs and signals we all use when we communicate with others. Part Two: Interactive Dialogue, helps us put together the individual concepts presented in the Part One, and helps us deal with people once we know body language. Part Three: Manipulating Dialogue provides us with some valuable information as to what we can do in an interview, meeting, or negotiation to ensure our body language is allowing us to maintain control.

Just as certain people can learn, or "pick up," spoken languages faster than others, the same is true for learning how to learn to read body language. Some of us pick up on the dialect of facial expressions while others notice body positioning. This is normal and with practice, we can all become proficient at understanding other dialects of *The Unspoken Dialogue*.

Part One

BODY LANGUAGE

UNDERSTANDING BODY LANGUAGE

In any face-to-face meeting there exists an almost impenetrable wall of uncertainty built on the unknown. What is in the mind of the other individual? What will they attempt to do? Will it be all verbal or will there be physical confrontation? Neither party can predict what will occur in the next few seconds.

In a momentary, sweeping glance, you must identify the key areas of the other individual's body: the eyes, the arms, the hands, and the feet. Their position can reveal what you need to know so you can prepare yourself for any personal action. Do not assume or anticipate what your opponent will do. Do not concentrate on the ravings of the mouth. Learn to understand the more complex message the body is telegraphing.

Definition of Terms

To place the concepts into a perspective that will be easier for us to understand, we will break them down into three categories: neutral, defensive, and aggressive.

Neutral - The neutral person is between the position of defensive and aggressive. They exhibit little or no emotion. They are in an open state of mind and almost seem "relaxed." They do not feel threatened and are not trying to seek an advantage.

When a person is neutral they are open to receiving and giving information. When you ask them a question they will answer it without hesitation, and when given information they will discuss it without emotion. When a person exhibits neutral body language they are the most accepting of new ideas and concepts.

Defensive - The defensive person is resistant. It is as if every step is blocked. It could be that they are resistant to you as an individual, what you have said to them, or what you have asked them to do.

Neutral

They could also be resistant to you simply for what you represent to them.

Body Language

When a person is defensive, information has to be pulled out of them. It is a verbal tug-of-war. When you ask a question, they refuse to answer, either by lying or not answering. They cannot allow themselves to be vulnerable. They will not give or receive any information. They have adopted a totally static position.

Changes from defensive to aggressive are usually sudden. When you are dealing with a defensive person you should try to de-escalate the situation so the other person's attitude becomes more neutral. This will improve the circumstance for both of you.

Aggressive - This person is ready for action! You don't need to ask them anything. They're going to tell you exactly "what is what." They are agitated and ready for confrontation, either verbal or physical in nature.

Defensive

When a person becomes aggressive they become a one-way street. They will give you all the information they want you to have but will not accept any information you offer. Many times, in a group setting, they will not even hear the other people. They will talk over you or through you. Their mind is set to the point of obsession.

Be careful when dealing with an aggressive person. Verbal action often incites them to physical action. The thunderstorm of words often builds into a lightening bolt reaction. It is important to make sure your dialogue and body language are non-aggressive. If the individual is hostile or aggressive, continue with comments and actions that will guide the situation in a neutral direction.

Watch carefully for any changes in a person's body language! These signals can be very subtle and discrete, but extremely important. Make sure you remain calm and your body language remains neutral. It is the only way you will truly be in control.

Aggressive

> The Unspoken Dialogue

WHAT THE BODY IS SAYING

The Eyes

The eyes are the pathway the mind follows. Wherever the eyes are focused, so is the mind. When a person's eyes are wide open and looking at you, this could be seen as **neutral** body language. The path is open. This person will be receptive to your comments and more willing to give you information. The more a person's eyes are open, the more accepting they are of the information being presented. The extreme case of this is someone who is frightened. They will open their eyes as wide as possible to try to absorb as much visual knowledge as fast as possible to help them understand the situation.

Neutral

Neutral

Neutral

Body Language

When a person is avoiding eye contact with you, and is looking all over the area around you, this could be seen as **defensive** body language. This person is trying to block the pathway so you cannot receive information from them. Just as we open our eyes to let information in, we narrow our eyes or squint to keep information from getting out, thus hiding it from others.

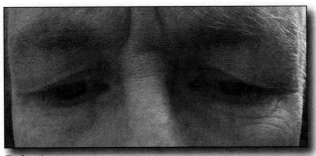
Defensive

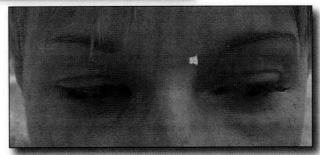
Defensive

Defensive

> The Unspoken Dialogue

When a person narrows their eyes but maintains direct eye contact with you, this could be seen as **aggressive** body language. In extreme cases, when a person is enraged, they will totally shut their eyes. It is as if they are trying to block the flow of any information in or out.

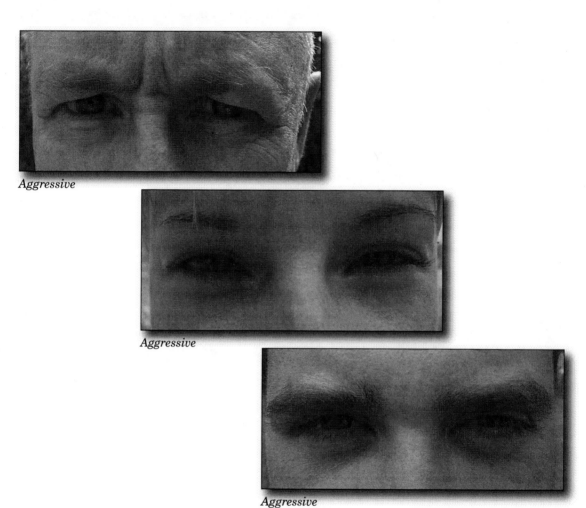

Aggressive

Aggressive

Aggressive

When someone is asked for information and their eyes look down as they answer, it is usually a truthful answer. When looking down, we are retrieving information from memory. It's as if we are reading the information off a piece of paper. This paper is not in our hands or on the desk - it's in our mind. Also, if someone is quoting memorized material you may even see the head move left to right as they "read" the information exactly how it was printed when they first learned it.

When you ask a person a question and they look up, they are usually lying. When a person creates or makes up a story it is a natural reaction to look up and even gaze off into the distance. Think about the last time you asked a small child what happened to the missing cookies. As adults, we still have the same body language as when we were children; it's just more subtle now.

Watch for eye movement that will tip you off to "secrets." When you ask, "Where are the drugs," the verbal answer may be, "I don't know," but as they answer, they glance at their friend's jacket pocket. There is a good chance they have just given you more information than they wanted you to have. This type of eye movement is quick and usually done unconsciously. It is not a matter of intelligence; it is simply the subconscious mind betraying the person.

Be prepared to protect yourself from an individual who is continually glancing at or openly staring at a specific area of your body, such as your hands or feet. They may be formulating a plan to take physical control of the situation away from you. Also, be prepared to act if a person is staring at a concealed area nearby - their briefcase, desk drawer, or any other area where there might be a hidden object that could be used against you.

> The Unspoken Dialogue

The Head

When a person's head is resting evenly in balance on their neck, this could be seen as **neutral** body language. When the person's head is leaning back, trying to create a greater distance between the two of you, this could be seen as **defensive** body language. When a person's head is leaning forward, this could be interpreted in two ways: The individual could be seeking more information by having closer contact with you or with what you are saying. This is an example of non-confrontational aggression. They could also be trying to intimidate you. Both cases are considered **aggressive** body language because the individual wants to take some form of action.

Neutral

Defensive

Aggressive

Body Language

The Arms

The position of an individual's arms can forecast possible action. Arms fully extended and hanging relaxed at a person's side generally indicate a relaxed frame of mind. When seated, the arms would be resting on the arms of the chair, or on the table in front of them. These could both be seen as **neutral** body language. When a person's arms are folded across their chest, it usually denotes insecurity, fear, or defiance. This could be seen as **defensive** body language. When the arms are tense and the elbows are bent, this raises the hands above the waist. If the person is seated, the hands will be above the table. Whether the hands are open or clenched in a fist, their arms could be considered to be in **aggressive** body language.

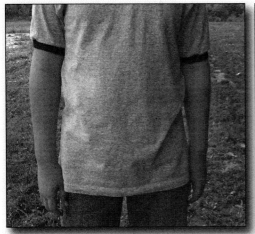
Neutral

Defensive

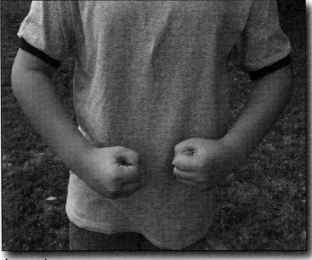
Aggressive

> The Unspoken Dialogue

The Hands

When a person's hands are open and relaxed, their arms at their sides or resting on the table in front of them, this could be considered **neutral** body language. When a person is constantly moving their fingers or shifting their hands from the table top to their lap and back again, this could be seen as a nervous gesture or **defensive** body language.

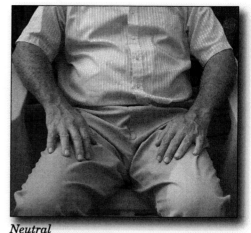
Neutral

When a person's hands are clenched into fists or they are opening and closing their hands repeatedly, this is usually viewed as **aggressive** body language.

There are times, however, when a person will be so overcome with emotion, they will clench their fists. Extreme fear causes us to tighten all muscles. If they don't have someone else to grab, an individual will pull their arms in close to their body and squeeze their hands shut as tight as possible. Extreme joy causes athletes around the world to thrust their fist up in the air in a triumphant gesture. Politicians will pump their fists to emphatically drive a point home. In all cases, the emotions are extreme and the hands are clenched in fists.

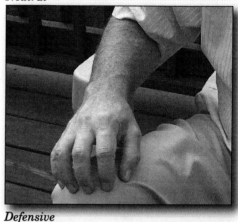
Defensive

The position of the hands can also be an indication as to whether or not an individual intends to take action against you. Hands on the hips are usually **defensive** or defiant,

Aggressive

similar to arms folded across the chest. Hands behind the back can send very mixed signals. If the person has a military background, this is a signal that they are at ease in your presence and it would be **neutral** body language, however, this could also be an individual who is trying to hide something from you. Be very careful when you see hands behind the back. It is best to consider "the total picture" of body signs and weigh all of them for a more accurate interpretation.

Body Language

The Feet

Whether a person is standing or seated, the feet can tell a lot about their attitude. If someone is standing with their body weight evenly distributed on both feet and neither foot is predominately forward, this could be seen as relaxed, **neutral** body language. When a person is leaning back, and the majority of their body weight is on their heels, this could be **defensive** body language. In order to make a quick attack, an individual needs to redistribute body weight over the front area or balls of his feet. This makes them more mobile so they can run from you or lunge forward at you. When a person is leaning forward on the balls of their feet, this could be seen as **aggressive** body language.

When a person is seated, the placement of their feet can be just as important as when they are standing. When the legs are positioned so the bottoms of both feet are on the floor and the lower legs are perpendicular to the chair, this could be **neutral** body language. When a seated person positions their feet directly between themselves and an individual they are having a dialogue with and crosses their legs, this could be **defensive** body language. When an individual places their feet under the chair so that their toes are making contact with the floor, causing them to lean forward as if they are about to stand up, this could be seen as **aggressive** body language.

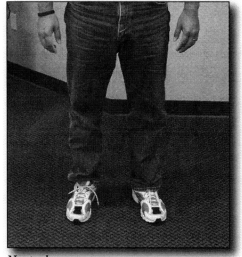
Neutral

Defensive

Aggressive

> The Unspoken Dialogue

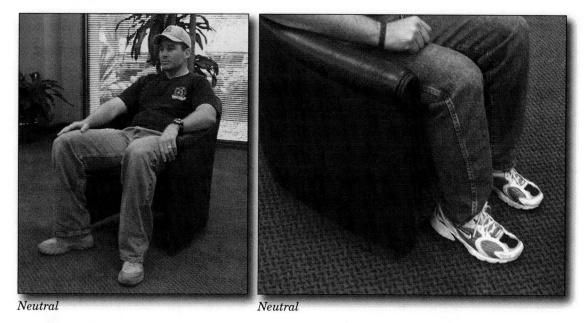

Neutral   *Neutral*

If, during a discussion with someone, you observe the other person suddenly shift one of their feet back to a position under their chair, it may indicate that their attitude about what is being discussed has changed and they have moved to a more **aggressive** position. If it is a group discussion, the individual that has been silent may be gesturing that they now want to be more active in the dialogue. Try to remember what was said to evoke this reaction as this information might be helpful in future discussions; it can help you manipulate not only the conversation, but also the attitudes of the people involved.

Defensive   *Defensive*

Mildly Defensive

Extremely Defensive

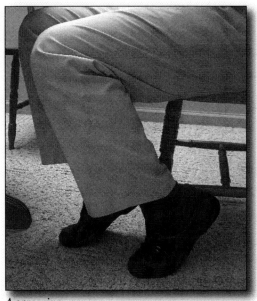
Aggressive

Another piece of information that can be determined from foot placement is whether a person is right or left handed. Usually, a person will put their "strong side" foot (right foot if they are right handed - left foot if they are left handed) further back for more power. This is an instinctive response so even if a person is not a "trained fighter" they can react in this manner. When seated, if someone becomes more **aggressive** in their speech or attitude, they change their footing, placing their strong side back, getting ready for action. Be very cautious if a person changes their foot position! This most always signals impending action.

It is important to remember that the most reliable and consistent method for understanding nonverbal messages is combining several body gestures. There will be times when you will see individuals who are between the categories or are displaying mixed messages. This is quite normal when you factor in all our individualities and cultural differences.

> The Unspoken Dialogue

EXAMPLES OF BODY LANGUAGE

Example One

You are about to interview a person who is sitting in a chair with their hands open and their arms resting on the table in front of them. They are looking right at you with their eyes wide open and their head is balanced between their shoulders.

This person is?

Neutral

Defensive

Aggressive

Example Two

As the interview progresses, this person starts to lean back in the chair, crosses their legs and folds their arms across their chest. Their head leans back and instead of looking at you as you speak, they start looking around the room, avoiding eye contact, even when speaking to you.

This person is?

Neutral

Defensive

Aggressive

Example Three

Further into your interview, this individual starts leaning forward in their seat, with their feet under the chair and their body leaning forward. Their hands are clenched shut and their eyes are narrowed, looking right at you.

This person is?

Neutral

Defensive

Aggressive

Now that you are aware of the non-verbal messages others send, it is important for you to consider the body signals you are presenting. In most situations, you should make a constant and concerted effort to maintain neutral body language. Your actions can de-escalate a situation and guide a potentially aggressive scenario to a peaceful conclusion.

HAND GESTURES
What the hands are saying

Some people use their hands a great deal when they are talking, while others are much less animated and use their hands very little. The one thing that is consistent is that we all talk with our hands. It is one of the most constant physical displays of body language used throughout the world. People will even use their hands while talking when there is no one else present. Have you ever caught yourself using hand gestures while you were rehearsing a speech by yourself or talking on the telephone? Hand gestures supplement verbal communication and many times the person speaking does not realize these gestures are being used. These gestures can be very informative and are often more reliable than the words being spoken. Most hand gestures can be divided into three basic groups, displayed at different levels of intensity. They are palm up, palm down, and the palm facing the person being spoken to or vertical palm.

The **palm up** gesture is displayed as a supplement to verbal conversation to emphasize the comments being presented, such as "it was a lot of work . . ." or "Wow, that's bright." The palm up is also used when you are asking for or receiving information. Just as you turn hand palm up to receive an object, you turn your hand up to take in information. Questions such as "Do you agree?" or "Will you allow them . . ." cause us to turn our hands to a receiving position. Normally this gesture is not used with a demand or when speaking in an authoritative tone. When we are seeking cooperation and requesting information the hands are palm up.

The **palm down** gesture is displayed as the reverse of the palm up gesture. It is shown as a supplement to forceful conversation or added as emphasis to an order or command. The words that accompany this hand signal are usually blunt and precise such as "Get out of the office!" or "We will

be at that meeting." A statement made with direct verbal force usually includes other body signs as well as the hand gestures. When a person points their finger, even though most of the fingers are folded back, when this motion is being done for emphasis or to demand action, the palm is down.

The **vertical palm** is the universal "stop sign". Whether it is an index finger on the lips to silently ask someone to stop talking or an arm extended with the palm displayed to tell a motorist to stop his vehicle, the message is clear. The individual using this gesture is in a position to regulate the flow of the actions or conversation taking place and something must cease.

The vertical palm is a commonly displayed gesture in a meeting or group situation. The person who utilizes this gesture is assuming the position of leader and will try to maintain control of others involved. It is important to observe the level of intensity or how emphatically this gesture is displayed. This information can tell you the amount of authority the person has in that group. If a person achieves control with a slight and rather relaxed gesture, this individual is one who has command of the scene without the need to "over display." This person is also more apt to be quiet in their speech and in control of all around them.

If, however, the reverse is true and you are observing someone with a lower confidence level who is trying to appear more impressive and important to those around them, most body language, especially hand gestures, will become more bold and flagrant. The volume level also becomes pronounced and the words themselves more staccato.

Raising one's hand to ask permission to speak is a vertical palm gesture. The person who raises a hand wants to speak and is asking everyone else in the group to stop the discussion and listen to them. It may start with the hand at shoulder height - a polite interruption in the conversation - but it can quickly escalate into a waving flag at arm's length, overhead, "yelling" for recognition.

> The Unspoken Dialogue

When you observe a group of people from a distance and cannot hear what is being said, body language and hand gestures can be an important means of obtaining knowledge of the situation. Who is giving the orders? Who is asking for direction? Is anyone in the group more agitated? If you can be more aware of what you are about to encounter, you will have better control of the situation and lessen the possibility of aggression against you.

No Leader

Definite Authority / Leader

EXTREME CIRCUMSTANCES

If you are in contact with a person who has been subjected to physical or mental torture you will usually perceive a drastically altered response. People who have been beaten or severely injured can become totally drained or "bleached" of all normal gestures, both aggressive and defensive; their body language is mute.

Movies, television, and the entertainment industry have given us a false image of the normal response of a person who has been emotionally devastated by an incident or event. They often display the person as being extremely "hyper," overly expressive, and at a high level of reactive gestures. In most cases, this will not be true. You will notice that the response to any questioning will be extremely diminished. They will usually display little if any emotion, even to questions that should normally evoke an aggressive response. All accompanying hand and facial gestures will be muted. They will appear to be exhausted and depleted of energy. They appear to be without emotion when, in reality, they are in deep need of professional care that should be encouraged without delay.

When a person has been a victim of an extreme circumstance, they rarely show open hostility toward their abuser. Open displays and threats against an aggressor are usually made by an interested third party, not the victim.

Any body language that does surface in a person who has been tortured or witnessed an incident of torture first hand will normally be neutral. Any gestures or emotions will usually be at a consistent level - no ups or downs. There will be little change of expression or emotion throughout your entire dialogue. Most of the information you amass will be through observation and not interaction.

Part Two

INTERACTIVE DIALOGUE

THE CONVERSATIONAL DISTANCE

Imagine that, between you and the person to whom you are speaking, there is a space into which your words fit. During most conversations, the entire dialogue takes place with one, established distance from the start of the discussion to its end. But when the emotional level changes, so does the space between those involved.

Various cultures have different amounts or degrees of "personal space". What is important for us to observe is not the distance a conversation begins at, but the fluctuations of the distances between the parties while they are talking. This will give us a better understanding of the dynamics of the dialogue as we see it unfold before us. It will help us understand the importance of what has been said.

When a person is aggressive or has strong emotional feelings about what is being said, they will lean forward to compress the area their words have to travel. Also, when the item being discussed is of a personal or private nature, the person will have a tendency to lean into their words.

When a person is speaking, but is defensive, and thinks their comments will be met with a negative reaction, many times they will anticipate the aggressive response by leaning or stepping back as they speak to avoid having the conversational distance compressed. If they feel their comments will be met with a positive response, they will lean forward or step in closer in anticipation of acceptance of their point of view.

Interactive Dialogue

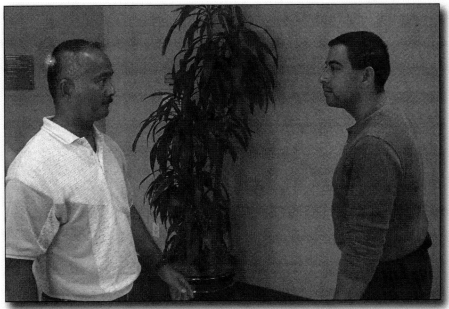
Aggressive

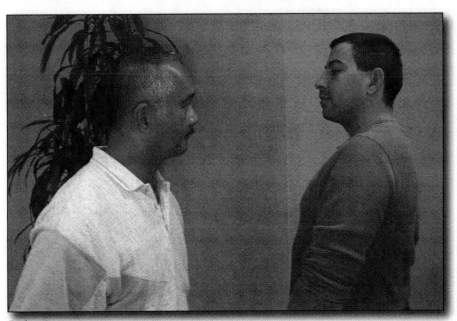
Defensive

> The Unspoken Dialogue

When two individuals meet, the contact distance that quickly becomes established can tell us more than the verbal greetings being exchanged. If two people have had prior contact that was of a negative nature, the distance between them will be greater than the distance established between two friends. Another reliable gesture of body language that often accompanies this is whether or not the eyes narrow as the individuals extend their arms for a handshake or other traditional greeting. Narrowed eyes are a sign that the person being met is not being accepted or possibly trusted.

Friend or Foe?

Interactive Dialogue

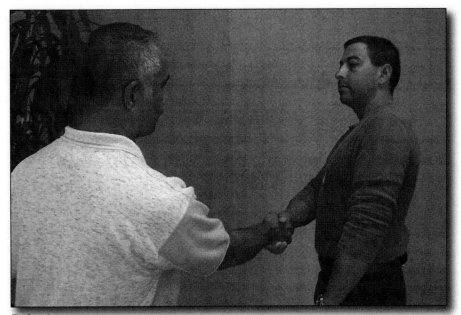
Defensive

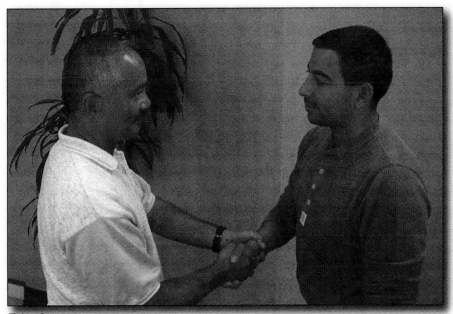
Friends

– 43 –

THE VOLUME FACTOR

The volume of our speech can be a vital key to our emotional state. Many times, we react to volume keys without even realizing it. Consider the common phrases we all use in our daily lives - "three cheers for the winner," or "a moment of silence, please." The circumstance in which a person perceives themselves to be will be a major contributing factor to the volume and pitch of their voice.

Be aware of any subtle changes in the volume, speed, or pitch of a person's voice as they speak. It can reveal what they feel is of greater importance to the circumstance at hand. The volume generated by a person in a conversation with one or more other persons will rise and fall in direct proportion to how important they think their comments are to the meeting.

When a person is aggressive, they will raise their voice and become louder. This can be to emphasize a point in a discussion or it can be in the form of a shout to a friend across a crowded room.

When an individual is agitated or emotional, the speech will not only become louder, it will also become faster. When a person is seeking to achieve control of the situation, the language of the dialogue will become louder but the cadence will usually slow down and become more deliberate.

When a person is defensive, the volume can be more subdued or quiet. Their cadence will usually be slower, as if they are thinking about every word before they say it. A common defensive speech pattern is when someone mumbles. This is slowing the words and dropping the volume to a point where the words become inaudible.

What we must seek to do, under most circumstances, is to keep our volume level consistent. When needed, yield the floor to those who are eager to "tip their hand" with comments they never intended to make. Whether it is a social gathering or a business conference, be aware of not just what is being said, but how it is being said. The hidden meanings can be of great value to you when trying to assess the situation.

CONFRONTATIONAL POSITIONING

Confrontational Positioning refers to the stance and body placement an individual assumes when coming into contact with one or more other persons. The position that is taken can display the safety status of you or others, authority level, or acceptance within the structural group.

When a person or group of people is willing to accept you and they are in a non-confrontational position, they will face you and be toward the front of your body so you can see them. If you observe a group of people from a distance and everyone seems to be facing one individual, that person is probably the "leader" of the group. At that point in time, that person has the most authority and influence on the activities of that group.

Non-confrontational Group

> The Unspoken Dialogue

When a group of people is not willing to accept someone into their trust or if the situation is escalating into an aggressive condition, the people will try to encompass the "outsider." This will limit that individual's ability to monitor everyone else's actions. It will make the group feel superior and more in control. If you are in a situation where you feel a group of individuals is trying to establish an aggressive position behind your back or out of your view, try to physically step back, keeping the majority of the group where it can be observed for any action against you.

Encompassing the "Outsider"?

Just as with animals, humans will try to protect the weak and the old by placing them in the center of the group. An important person or someone with authority will also be protected by the gathering. Do not assume the person at the head of the crowd is the one who is in charge. Watch the body language of the rest of the people to determine who the most important one is.

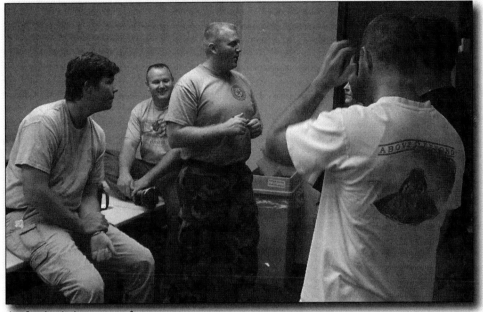

Authority is in center of group

> The Unspoken Dialogue

ESCALATING AGGRESSION

Escalating aggression, such as a person "losing control," is a common circumstance or condition that becomes clearly understandable once you are aware of body language and gestures.

In the beginning of this book we dissected the gestures and body language that people display into three basic areas: neutral, defensive, and aggressive. When we are dealing with an escalation of emotions or aggression, the most important factor to be aware of, as stated before, is change! In a circumstance where there is "aggression escalation," the person or persons may display neutral body language and change to aggressive behavior, or they may display defensive body language and change to aggressive behavior. This escalation may also include the compression of the conversational distance and an increase in the volume and/or pitch of their voice.

Once an individual has escalated to the use or display of aggressive body language and has "no where else to go" to vent their anger or frustration, the aggressive gestures become compounded. The same gesture or phrase is repeated over and over, many times in a rhythmic, staccato pattern. When this occurs, you should consider the fuse to be lit.

Neutral start

Anyone can physically attack at any time, but when a person escalates to repeated gestures of aggressive body language, the next step is almost always a physical outburst. They may strike at an inanimate object, such as kicking the desk or punching the wall, or they will strike at another person. The only other option, rarely chosen, is to run away; escape.

Our role in the de-escalation of this situation is to remain neutral in our gestures and actions. It is human nature to act defensive ("Peace at all cost"), or aggressive ("I'll show you who's in charge"), but both of these options will only add to the confusion and aggression that is building in the mind of the other person. Remember, the best confrontation you'll ever have is the one you just avoided. Never place yourself or others in an unsafe circumstance in these situations by being defensive or aggressive. Your calm and controlled display of neutral gestures will be far more effective than the collision of aggressive actions from both sides.

The escalation begins

> The Unspoken Dialogue

Physical contact

Physical escalation response

THE FRIENDLY ATTACK

Why do people compromise what was once a totally inflexible demand? Why do they suddenly yield to a different point of view or request? Could it be that we all place a higher priority on the body language we see in others than we realize? Can these gestures be used to help us achieve our goals?

When an individual is involved in a form of personal contact with others, whether it is casual and random, or well planned but difficult, body language clearly reflects the intent and substance of the words being spoken. If we are to successfully manipulate the dialogue, we need to learn how to control body language and "say" what we want with discrete gestures.

When a person is displaying neutral body language and gestures, they will be open to suggestions and willing to compromise. When the body language becomes defensive, even if it appears that they are listening to what you are saying, their mind could be busy thinking of strategies to stop you from changing their mind and they may not be receptive to your ideas. When a person is aggressive, they will go beyond being close minded and demand their own way. They can be so caught up in the moment that they will refuse your suggestion, even when it is simply a restatement of their own demand, such as a person refusing a half dozen pieces of something because they demanded six of them.

When a person is in a defensive or aggressive posture, do not expect them to change their way of thinking to your ideas. They need to relax their state of mind to be open to new concepts. When a person is defensive, they are usually trying to think of a counter measure to what you are proposing. This is the time the discussion can be swayed off the main topic to side issues that are irrelevant. Be careful not to be lead off course or to let your body language take the deliberations in a direction they need not go.

How do we keep people neutral and receptive to our concepts? We must remain neutral ourselves. Allow the other side to speak its mind but make sure your body language remains neutral, even if your emotions do not. After they have stated what they want, they will see your gestures and be more likely to remain neutral and open to your ideas. If your reactions become defensive, they will become defensive, and the entire discussion will become mired down in negative feelings. Instead of working towards a compromise, both sides will become frustrated with the situation.

You can only feed your requests to someone who is willing to listen to them. By continuing to display neutral body language, you lessen the tendency of others to slip into a defensive state of mind, and allow for an environment where they will be more susceptible to the perspective you are placing before them.

GESTURES
The "Missing Link" to Understanding

"What did they mean by that remark?" "Did you hear what they just said?" How many times in your life have you heard those comments, or even made them yourself? We have all been in situations where words alone were not enough to understand the situation developing around us. Let's consider this example – a letter is slid under your door at work that reads:

"Dear Friend,

After having worked with you for one long year several of us want to meet you at the restaurant around the corner so we can clearly express how we feel about you. Considering all you've done we want to make sure that you get everything that's coming to you. After all – you deserve it! Don't be later than six. We can't start without you."

If you received that note, would you want to go to that restaurant? Without the aid of physical gestures it can be extremely difficult to determine the "true" meaning of what is being said to us.

Not all body language is as blatant as a cheerleader on the sidelines of the big game. Gestures that include movement of a person's arms or the full body are easily detected, but watch closely for the more subtle movements that are displayed when someone is talking to you, especially when it is a "one-on-one" conversation. When you display the appropriate body language, even if the person to whom you are talking is a complete stranger, they might confide in you as if you were a long time friend.

Gestures You Observe	What The Gestures Mean
Eyes looking down	Remembering information.
Deep breath or a sigh	Grief, disappointment, deep thought.
Leaning toward you	Personal or serious thought to follow.
Speech begins to slow	Important information.
Words pronounced more crisply	Important information.
Hands in contact with your hands	Sincere.
Holding the palms of their hands together	Sincere.
Arms and legs "pulled in" to body	Information too personal, defensive.

Gestures You Should Display	How To Communicate This
Neutral eyes and head position	Look at the person talking. *What they're saying is important to you.*
Neutral stance	Don't lean back (defensive posture). Don't lean forward (aggressive posture).
Neutral hands	Hands are at your side if standing. Hands in your lap or on armrests if seated.
Neutral leg position	Weight evenly distributed if standing. Legs not crossed above the knee if seated.

The one gesture that will stop a conversation in its tracks is the tapping of an extremity: tapping you foot on the floor, tapping your fingers on the table or arm of the chair, shaking your leg up and down. This is a sign that you are bored or in a hurry. You might as well just ask the other person to stop talking because that is how they will interpret your physical gesture.

It is very important to show neutral body language and gestures throughout any dialogue with others. When you look "at" them, make sure it is not just a blank stare; that you are not looking down at them or narrowing your eyes in an aggressive motion. If your body language projects even a small amount of sincerity, you are much more likely to get information from the other person.

Part Three

MANIPULATING DIALOGUE

CONTROL
Are You In Control?

Our initial contact with others is almost always a determining factor in control. First impressions are part of human nature and play a very important part in how we react with others. There is a reason most people think large and powerful athletes are not as intelligent as the studious, frail individuals who spend all their free time in the library. We have been conditioned to believe that the well-dressed person is more honest and knowledgeable than the beggar on the corner, just as we have been taught that people in authority always speak the truth. We all have the tendency to oversimplify a situation by putting a singular attribute on people we meet.

In any dialogue with another person, under any circumstance, the more weight or respect we give to that person's position, the more weight or respect we give their words. Throughout the world, people in authority announce their station by way of their appearance. Tribal chiefs wear robes and headdresses. Courtroom judges wear dark robes and we are told to stand when they enter the room. Almost always, the person in authority sits higher than the people "being judged." When dealing with others we need to create "a role" that shows confidence and authority but maintains respect. Always remember, the image that others have of us in their minds, whether it is correct or not, is a determining factor in our control of the conversation.

To be blunt, we need to maintain control. We must control our emotions, our actions and the situations in which we are involved. Remember, even a mob has a leader. We need to stay focused and well grounded no matter what is occurring around us. We cannot seek to control or manipulate the other side of the conversation if we do not have control in our own team. The leadership of the team of which you are a member must be better than the leadership of those across the table from you.

Control can take place in many forms. It can be extremely subtle and discrete, such as controlling the temperature of the room or the time of the meeting to better suit your personal needs. Control can be blatantly obvious, even to the point of being insulting and dictatorial. Maintain control, but do not cause the opposition to become defensive and unresponsive.

Control the direction of the interactive dialogue. Guide the participants in the appropriate direction to seek out a solution to the problem that brought you and/or your teams together. Always remember, we can talk about having a balance of authority and decision making power in mediation and negotiation situations, but when you have a certain objective or goal, it is preferable to have that balance in your favor. Discrete control can achieve this goal without offending the other groups involved.

The organization and leadership skills you display by maintaining personal control will help your team achieve its goals and keep the discussion focused on the objectives that need to be addressed.

CHANGING THEIR DIRECTION
Keeping The Dialogue Flowing

You are trying to talk to an individual and the only responses you are receiving are defensive or nonexistent. You've done your best to make sure your body language is neutral but the other person remains totally closed and defensive. What can you do? Is the interview over or can you manipulate the uncooperative body language into compliant interaction.

People display defensive body language when they are uncomfortable with a situation. The more uncomfortable they are the more compound these defensive gestures become. They fold their arms and step or lean back to create distance. They tuck their legs under their chair so their feet are not exposed. It is a natural defensive gesture to pull back from danger or the unknown. Defensive body language can escalate to aggressive behavior very quickly. Body language reflects a person's state of mind, and a person's state of mind dictates their body language. People are protective not only of themselves, but also of their knowledge and information. We need to make them feel comfortable enough to talk to us by maneuvering their body language from defensive or aggressive to neutral.

> The Unspoken Dialogue

If the person has their arms folded, offer them something in a way that forces them to reach for it. If a person has their hands in a fist, give them something to hold. You cannot drink a cup of coffee with your arms crossed. You cannot hold a glass of water when your hand is in a fist. Give the person a piece of paper and a pencil so they can make notes, but don't put it directly in front of them. Place the paper a short reach away. This will force the individual to uncross their legs as they lean forward and transition from a totally defensive body posture to one that is more open and receptive.

If a person is looking away from you, give them something to look at. Put a non-confrontational picture on the table. Their eyes are now focusing on a neutral item. Encourage them to pick up the picture. Once again, they will have to lean forward to reach it; the arms uncross, the body moves forward, and they are more open to what is happening around them.

If an individual is standing or pacing back and forth, encourage them to write down information they feel could be helpful to them. It is a natural reaction to want to sit when we write. Have paper, pencil, and an open chair available where you want them to sit. Let them think that they are assuming some personal level of control.

Once the person starts to change their body language, give them a folder or an envelope for their papers. They now have something tangible that is theirs. It doesn't matter how small the item is, they are now more likely to be willing to give you information. Think about the last time you went to a bank or dealt with someone in any professional situation for the first time. They gave you a pen or a business card, and when they said you could keep it, you thanked them. You had received something and were more at ease to give them information.

The most constant relationship between humans is give and take. Whether it is one-on-one or groups of people, we all want to feel like we gained something from a situation. By maneuvering people to neutral body language we are allowing them to interact, and opening the door for what could be a very useful dialogue.

THE GROUP
Many as One

When we are trying to categorize a person by their body language, we look at all their gestures. The dominate gestures tell us what we need to know about that individual. When we are dealing with a group of people we need to do the same thing. We look at the entire group to determine their attitude.

A group should be treated as a single entity. One member may have a different opinion, but the mind set of the majority will be the way the "team" reacts. Scan the group for the most common or dominate body language. Are they confident and walking into the meeting with their heads up and eyes narrow, ready for the "battle" ahead; or is there one person who is ready and the rest of the group is slowly following, looking down or reading notes.

It is human nature to want to be part of a group. We all feel safer when we are not alone. It is also human nature for our attitudes and body language to become more aggressive when we feel we have been accepted by the group. This is why fans at sporting events react differently than they would if they were watching the game at home and why we use the phrase "mob mentality" to explain certain behavior.

Some groups will have a definite leader. Other members of the team will try to emulate the leader's attitude which means they will also try to copy the gestures and body language of the person they feel is in charge. Whether it is on a football field or in a boardroom, the person that has the most positive attitude is chosen as team leader. It is important for us to be able to determine who the leader is if we are going to be able to control the team. Once we have the leader agreeing with our mindset the rest of the group will follow.

THE AGENDA
Better Yours Than Theirs

Do not be confused or frightened by the word "agenda." To put this concept into a simple definition, think of it as a list of things that both sides of a deliberation want to openly discuss at the meeting table. The list may be extremely brief or it can be quite extensive and involved.

Whether a relationship is predicated on a written document or a casual handshake, it needs to be carefully developed and reinforced with trust. Great care should be taken to make sure any list or agenda contains items that are of interest to all concerned. This will help to ensure that everyone will become involved in the meeting and negotiations.

Be aware of the basic concept of the "good vs. bad" agenda. Simply put – our agenda is good for us—their agenda is good for them which could make it bad for us. This perspective may seem a bit ruthless or downright inconsiderate at first glance, but it is important to hold to your own perspective throughout the negotiations. Be careful not to win ground at the bargaining table only to loose footing at the final agreement.

Respectfully solicit written items for an agenda. Encourage both sides of any negotiation to feel that they are an equal part of the meeting and process. Remember though, that whenever you put something in writing and give it to someone else, there is a good chance you will have to live with it. However, and quite properly so, when the opposition puts something forward in its written agenda, they too can be held accountable.

THE OTHER TEAM

The very first contact you have with another group or team has the potential for being incredibly enlightening about the inner workings of that team. Use this first contact as an understanding phase that you build on for a future advantage. Don't be so caught up in the big picture of the mediation process that you loose sight of the small yet critically important details. Be aware of how all the interpersonal complexities being displayed relate to each other – and to you!

Before you sit down and introduce yourself at a first meeting, take note of certain characteristics of the other group. Are they a unified team? Does one person seem to be in charge, telling the rest of the group where to sit or how to act? Is someone passing out notes or papers? Is that person the quiet worker or the person in charge?

Be aware of any questions they ask you or other members of your team? Do they want to know who the "team leader" is? They will not ask this question unless their team has a definite authority figure. Make sure any information they give you during their personal introductions agrees with the body language expressed before the meeting began. Make note of who is the most outgoing and aggressive during these introductions. This person may be the easiest to negotiate with during the meeting.

Watch for any fracturing of their "unified front." Are they working together as a team or does it appear that there are small cliques trying to work together? Conflicts within a team can be caused by legitimate problems, but they can also surface over very frivolous items. As you watch the other team for "the chink in their armor," make sure your own team is not dividing over petty issues.

BASIC PERSONALITY TYPES YOU MAY ENCOUNTER

Amid the multitude of people we will have the pleasure and displeasure of dealing with, no two will be the same. However, they all exhibit some similarities and common traits when we interact with them. Keep this in mind as we examine some of the general characteristics of the different types of individuals we could encounter and how they might interact with us.

The Enthusiastic Misdirector

This is a person who generally appears to be highly self-motivated and interested in every word spoken by any and all people. They have the tendency to be overly interactive with comments and questions and, with total spontaneity, they can and will, take over the meeting or conversation by providing an endless flood of commentary. They classically will talk more and more about less and less until they have said everything there is to say about nothing.

> The Unspoken Dialogue

Body Language

The Enthusiastic Misdirector will exhibit wide open eyes that seem to spend more time rambling around the room than making direct eye contact with whoever is speaking. They generally are leaning forward in their chair in anticipation of adding to the discussion. Their arms will be resting on the table or placed in their lap in a relaxed manner. They spend most of their time speaking with their palms up, directing their comments to everyone in the area in a routine manner. They do not acknowledge anyone as an authority or team leader.

Solution

There is no polite, socially acceptable, or otherwise gracious way to intercede in this onslaught of verbal commentary, so just interrupt. As long as it is done with a smile on your face and a "thank you for bringing that up", or "Let's get back to OUR agenda", you can usually regain control without offending the Misdirector. You can compliment them but make sure you display aggressive gestures to show control while doing it. You may have to become quite assertive with your body language - even confusing the Misdirector by displaying aggressive gestures when stating neutral comments. If it becomes a severe problem, call for a brief recess. After the break, guide the meeting back in the direction it needs to go by immediately setting forth a new proposal or refer back to the agenda. The main point is that you must maintain control of the meeting and keep it going in a direction that will benefit your team.

The Quiet Ambusher

This is the person who sits back throughout the meeting and lets others make statements, ask questions, and develop the strengths and openings for their side during the debate process. They may or may not be diligently taking notes in a physical manner but be assured that they are quite aware of the topics and direction of the conversation. Some ambushers are interested in the entire dialogue of the meeting, however, most will be lying in wait for the moment their area of concern or topic of interest is introduced and commented on. Remember one extremely important trait about the ambusher - they seldom ask any questions to which they do not already know the answers! Their interest in this meeting is strictly to catch you off guard in a mistake or a lie. Their efforts are not to be dealt with lightly or brushed aside.

Body Language

The Quiet Ambusher will sit back in silence, making direct eye contact with everyone who speaks. The head movement will be limited, but the eye movement will be in a constant state of scanning all who offer a comment. Whether they are studiously leaning forward on the table, or in a relaxed "lean back in the chair" manner, in most cases, they will be taking notes on the conversation. One of the most unusual gestures this person will display is that they will ask a question with their palms down. We have said that this gesture is usually used to show force or direct a statement. Do not be confused by what appears to be a shift in body language. The words may be phrased in the form of a question but there is a definite statement being made. This forceful question can become a focal point or a major problem if not handled properly.

Solution

It is the nature of the Quiet Ambusher to gather strength and power from your mistakes. Their greatest power and ultimate goal is to catch you trying to cover up the inaccuracies or conflicts you make in your presentation and comments. If you are caught in a mistake that you can admit to and still survive the meeting, it is best, in most cases, to do just that. The mistake or untruth you side step and do not directly address will have a tendency to come back and haunt you at the most inopportune moments.

Make sure your body language remains neutral at all times. If you display defensive gestures when admitting a mistake, the Quiet Ambusher will "dig deeper" to try to find more errors. If you become aggressive, they have achieved their goal and you have lost control of the situation. In both cases, your credibility has been destroyed and your team's agenda has been compromised. Stay neutral.

If "the worst thing" happens and you find yourself in what appears to be an error, you have a limited range of temporary damage control techniques or relatable comments. "Let me get back to you on that point", or "let's get back to the agenda" may pacify the opposition for a brief while. If the debate starts to become heated, ask for a brief recess. If the confrontation seems to be aimed at one member of your team in a more personal manner, it may be best to have that member "called away" and replace them for the remainder of the conference.

The Meeting Interviewer

This person is more of an annoyance than the clever tactical problem the other types presented. The main negative contribution this person can provide is that if your side pays attention to this distractor, they will not be able to pay attention to the agenda and issues of the meeting.

The Meeting Interviewer can not only be a problem for your team, but for the other party of negotiators as well. There are several unfortunate traits that this "legend in their own mind" poses. One of the things they relish doing is being in charge of reading and, unfortunately, rereading the agenda. At any moment the entire conference room can be thrown into a yawning fit by the individual saying, "Let's look at this again . . ." Perhaps one of the most time consuming and boring efforts they make is the constant and incessant repeating of everything that is said. It is, of course, preceded by a comment such as "Let's see if I understand you" or "Oh! You mean . . .", and the list can go on and on . . . The only thing this person is missing is the background music and spotlight for the full enhancement of the unique abilities they think they have.

The amount of contribution this person makes to the meeting is minimal. There are times however, when a "Quiet Ambusher" from the other side will encourage this interviewer because as you become more aggravated with their repetitious behavior, you are more apt to make changes and errors in your statements.

Body Language

The Meeting Interviewer is deeply involved in the debate process and generally will focus their full attention on the person who is talking at all times, even if the person is on their side of the table. It is not unusual for their own team members to gesture to this individual to be quiet. Hand and eye motions will show they are equally annoyed with the interruptions. The Interviewer will usually be leaning forward at the table with wide eyes, constantly turning to face anyone that speaks. The majority of hand gestures displayed by this person will be flamboyant and palm up, asking and/or repeating everything said.

The Unspoken Dialogue

Solution

The solution to the problem the Interviewer presents is not difficult, but it is a team problem and requires a team solution. All group members must be consistent and state similar comments when challenged by this distraction. Politely but forcefully state, "Please don't interrupt my chain of thought", "Please wait until I am finished", "Please don't repeat what I have just said", or "It is a waste of OUR time to read that again". Notice, all of the above phrases are statements. We have not asked them to comment on anything. This would only give them the opportunity they are looking for to continue domination of the conversation. The goal we are seeking to achieve is their silence. The team's body language should remain aggressive toward the Meeting Interviewer, much in the same manner as it should be toward the Misdirector. You may not need as many comments to control the Meeting Interviewer, but the level of intensity may have to be more forceful.

DIALOGUE TO "THE AUTHORITY"
Who Do You Talk To?

Your time and effort will always be best spent when dealing with the person who is "in charge" of the meeting or conference you are attending. You do not want to be placed in the position of dealing with an assistant or a person who is second in command of any negotiations. Take control of the situation by manipulating or reading the physical signs that are being displayed by the other side and use them to your advantage.

The unofficial rules of "talk and respond" are established in the first few minutes of any contact with another person or group. If you have been advised through formal introduction or procedure as to who is in charge of the opposing team or group, then it is to your advantage to focus on that person directly. No matter which member of the other side asks your team a question, your response is directed to the person who is leading the other team. All of your team's responses and questions should be directed at this one individual.

To diffuse the opposition's verbal attack on your team, whenever a question is asked, it should be answered by different members of your team on an almost rotating basis. This will help keep the other team off balance and not allow them the comfort of knowing who is leading your group.

If the leader of the opposition is not introduced to you, the other side is making an effort to present a wall of defense to limit your level of effectiveness in the interchange. If this occurs, you must try to determine who is in charge so your team has a focal person. Trying to determine the leadership of the other side during the actual meeting can be rather difficult. Try to be prepared for the meeting early, and discretely observe the individuals who will be involved. This will allow you the opportunity of seeing the opposition in their unguarded moments. In any case, make note of who the other team is facing when they are talking. Are they standing, or are the chairs arranged, so they are facing one person? Which speakers are talking with their palms up and who is the one figure who is instructing the others with a palm down gesture? The actual conversation being spoken is not as important as their body language. You now know the individual they have chosen to be their leader for this meeting.

Be aware that the leadership role can appear to change during a discussion. If the subject matter diverts to a technical specialty, a member of the opposing team who is more qualified to answer those questions may try to step in and become the authority. Do not be swayed or lead off course. Continue to address the original leader as they will ultimately be the one to retain control.

When approaching the conference table, a good diversionary tactic for your team is to have it appear as if you have divided the leadership role. If the opposition has no one person to target, their attack will be diffuses over your entire team, thus making your team stronger.

This method of attack and counter attack is really quite simple. Your group focuses on one member of their team, and their efforts are defused on all the individuals of your team evenly. Your force and efforts are strongest when focused on one person or area of attack. A chain can bear great stress, but it was not designed to have one link bear the entire load.

WHAT DO THEY REALLY WANT?
Watching For The Subtle Signals

You are sitting in your "vehicle of conversation" at the "stoplight of interactive dialogue" watching the signals change, and not knowing when to proceed. Let us start to put together what we have learned and apply it to the question of "what do they really want?"

> The Unspoken Dialogue

As you and your fellow colleagues sit in uncertainty, watching the opposition, you will begin to notice some subtle and discrete signals that are now quite apparent to you. As their focus person, or group leader, begins to speak, you will become aware that you have a new methodology for understanding the "unspoken conversation" that is about to take place in front of you.

Visualize a picture of several members of a team sitting across from you at a meeting table. Some are fumbling through papers for notes they forgot to take. Another, looking up with a pencil in his mouth, is thinking about the vacation that is only three weeks away. And one other person, the focus leader, is reading off a list of requests and demands that you are now intently trying to concentrate on. As the list progresses, you are wondering which of these items is the most important and what you should be concentrating most of your energy toward. Which items are negotiable requests and which items are polite demands . . . and then, all of a sudden, you know! How did they convey this information to you? The waterfall of subtle signals said more than their spoken word.

As the person was reading off their list of items, you noticed a difference in the "whole person" by being aware of their involuntary expression changes and gestures. As the leader began to read a certain demand or request, you noticed a slight palm up gesture being displayed. They wanted your immediate approval of that item. You also noticed that the leader leaned forward in their chair and spoke just slightly louder as that point was presented. Their intent was quite clear. This was the item of greatest importance to them. Now your team was able to devise a strategy around this insight, and use this knowledge to better manipulate the discussion.

What if the opposite situation is occurring? What if you are the person reading off a list of demands and you want to know how the other team is going to accept your ideas? Which items will be agreed upon and which items will be met with resistance? Let us consider this scenario. You are reading along through your "wish list" of demands and requests when you come to an item that causes an obvious shift in body gestures from three out of the four people sitting across the table from you. The first person leans back in their chair and folds their arms across their chest. This is the classic defensive posture and this individual has just told you he does not agree with you on that issue. Another person on the other team shifts his body position toward his own leader and displays wide eyes and palms up. This person is not sure of how they should feel and they are asking the leader to direct their thinking. The leader hears what you have read and leans back. Not only do they fold their arms across their chest, they also cross their legs above the knees and narrow their eyes as they glare at their own associates. This person is saying that not only are they opposed to what has just been said, they want their teammates to be opposed to it too.

You must also be aware of the body language of members of your own team when you are in negotiation or conference setting. When you are in an intense verbal debate and you see an esteemed colleague look at the clock and let out a quiet sigh as they lean back, looking up at the ceiling, they have just told you, loud and clear, that they are through with this part of the meeting and whatever else is discussed means very little to them at this point in time.

Remember, as you read others, they are reading you. Body language can develop and change very quickly. Stay alert to the nonverbal communication that is occurring around you.

THE GESTURE MIRROR
Using Natural Reactions

When we are exposed to certain circumstances, we react in a very consistent and predictable manner. How many times have you started laughing with everyone else even though you had no idea what was funny? Have you ever tried not to yawn when someone else did? People have a tendency to become a part of what is happening around them, and there is in all of us, an acute susceptibility to the "contagion of gestures."

These natural reactions can be broken down into two categories, "reactive gestures" and "choice gestures." When someone yawns, we yawn. When someone scratches his or her arm, our arm starts to itch. We react to their stimulus.

> The Unspoken Dialogue

When we are in a group setting such as at a sporting event or a theater performance and someone starts to applaud, we applaud. If someone laughs, we laugh. We choose to be part of the group. It is our "choice" to participate in what is going on around us – or was it?

Human beings are pack animals. We all want to be "part of the group." We want our actions and gestures to be accepted by others. It is as if there is a need to mirror other people so we know that we "fit in" or belong.

These "trigger gestures" are commonly used by entertainers who claim they can "read your mind." They watch as their subject reacts to a series of questions. When they see a positive response to a vague question, the "mind reader" will then begin to focus on that line of questioning. They're not reading anyone's mind – they're reading a person's body language.

When I worked in law enforcement and had to interview a suspect, almost inevitably, at some point during the questioning the suspect would ask me, "How did you know that?" I would tell them that I could read the truth in their eyes. From that point on in the interview, when the suspect started to tell a lie, they would break eye contact with me. They would look away from me or even try to cover their eyes with their hands so I couldn't see their face.

The people who are most susceptible to trigger gestures are usually more susceptible to the influence or ideas of others. How is this applicable to us? When we enter into a dialogue with an individual, we will notice a need for that person to be part of "the group." They will mirror the body language or gestures of the leader so they feel like they belong and add to the strength and authority of the group.

If you are in a negotiation setting and you are having a difficult time with one of the members of the opposing team, watch that individual during your breaks or at times when the conditions are neutral. What do they do when they are relaxed? Is there a certain phrase or gesture they use when they are happy or cheerful? Is there any information you can gather that will make them more sympathetic to your cause or agenda? What body language tells you they are relaxed and open to new concepts?

When you are presenting a new item and you want them to agree with you, use neutral body language. Unconsciously, this will lessen their defenses and make them more open to your ideas. Bring up items you have in common and that are of concern to everyone. Use their gestures to present these ideas as well. When you finally state your demands, this borrowed body language can make them think the concepts presented were, at least in part, their own idea.

REACTING TO DISPLAYED GESTURES
Your Quiet Control

Going nowhere at top speed? Are you working hard at a meeting where you and your team feel like you are talking to people who are about as receptive as a brick wall? You just might be talking to a wall - a wall of opposition. You are trying to communicate with individuals who have constructed a barrier of gestures and body language to block you out. As long as they sit there unchallenged and unchanged, they will not agree to anything you present. You need to guide your team into open and receptive body language to get through the wall of anti-communication.

Why did the other group of negotiators become defensive so quickly? Your notes and papers are spread out all over in front of you, your arms are on the table and you're leaning forward in your seat. Your eyes are narrow and your gaze is fixed on the opposition leader. You are ready for battle. And a battle is just what you will get. The other group is leaning back in their seats; their arms are crossed and folded against their chests. They are looking down or around the room, anywhere so they don't have to make eye contact with you.

When we put all the body language in writing it becomes obvious at how aggressive our team appears to be. If not out of intimidation, the other team must act defensively just for survival. Any chance of interactive dialogue is lost.

How different would the situation be if we were to approach the bargaining table in a more relaxed manner? We still must be prepared and vigilant about our agenda but it is important to display a calm demeanor. We need to manipulate the other side into a gesture display that will entice them into the discussion, making it more beneficial for everyone. Lean back in your chair and make sure your arm gestures remain neutral. Keep your eye contact and facial expressions neutral but friendly. Slowly, you will see the members of the other team start to lean forward and enter into the discussion.

Just as you can change the gesture direction of one individual, you can change the gesture direction of a group. It can be as simple as a pitcher of water and glasses on the table. This allows their team "footing on the battlefield." The bargaining table must be an active zone, not a barrier. If they have a reason to lean forward and approach the table for something non-confrontational, they will be more likely to participate in the other activity across the table - your discussion! Have paper and pencils on the table for them. Also, there is nothing wrong with having snack food on the table. The more often they have to reach toward the table, the more active they are becoming. Make sure your team is also approaching the table for reasons other than to force their opinions or demands on others.

Do not expect an instant response from the opposition. It will take a little time for them to start to feel comfortable with you and your team, but slowly their wall of defense will start to crumble, and their body language will become more open or even aggressive.

If you have had previous contact or are familiar with a member of the other group and had a good relationship with them, their defensive posturing will usually break down faster. If the contact you had was of a negative nature, it may be longer before they take you back into their confidence.

The contents of the conversation in the beginning of a negotiation are of little importance. The main concern is that the other side of the table is open to your ideas and has been successfully lured into the dialogue they were resistant to. Encourage both sides to stay active throughout the negotiations to prevent the wall of defense from being rebuilt.

ONE ON ONE
Or One vs. One

As human beings, we need to communicate. We need to be heard and want to be understood. Even before we could speak, we made sure our needs were met. As infants, our only means of verbal communication was cooing and crying so we relied on gestures to get our message understood. As we learned to speak, we started listening more to words and stopped paying attention to gestures, but the gestures are still there! We have also been negotiators from birth. Some of our greatest triumphs at negotiation occurred when we were teenagers, struggling for that extra half-hour of freedom on Saturday night. When you put these two simple facts of human nature together, you can use them to your advantage when interviewing someone.

It's not just the CEOs of major companies or police investigators who need or can benefit from having good interviewing skills. Common, every day situations call for all of us to be able to tell if the person to whom we are talking is telling us the truth or trying to deceive us.

Interviews and interrogations on TV are full of bright lights, cigar smoke, and in-your-face yelling. In the real world, a lot more is accomplished when we remember to display neutral gestures and body language, and stay quietly in control of the situation.

So how can we tell if the person we're talking to is telling us the truth, trying to deceive us, or manipulating the facts? How do we distinguish "truthful" body language and gestures from "deceptive" language and gestures? In police work, there is a saying, "Good investigators ask questions to find the answers, but great investigators ask questions when they already know the answers." The good investigator tries to understand what happened. The great investigator tries to understand the person and then the situation.

This may sound like a complex procedure but it is really quite simple. We need to turn the person into a human "lie detector machine." Polygraphs tests are not wizardry. The person administering the test begins by asking you questions about things they already know such as your name and address. They watch how the machine records your reaction to those questions. Then, they ask you a question they don't know the answer to and see if the machine reacts in the same manner. You can do the same thing the lie detector machine does, but instead of using wires and electrical impulses, you will be watching gestures and the person's reactions.

During the course of your conversation with a person, ask several casual questions that you know the answers to. Allow the individual to answer these questions in a relaxed manner. Don't challenge them if they "stretch the truth." Instead, watch their body language. You are setting a benchmark for truth gestures you can use to measure and judge the answers to future questions. Observe closely any changes in the person's body language when they tell the truth or when they lie. Are they covering part of their mouth with their hands? Do they look away and break eye contact? There is a reason people say "Look me straight in the eye and say that." Watch for new gestures that emerge during the conversation. Are they deceptive gestures, defensive gestures? The more defensive an individual becomes, the greater the likelihood they will feel the need to protect the truth, or lie.

The important thing to remember is that you need to give the impression that you have plenty of time to talk to this person. Don't make them feel rushed. Casual conversation in the beginning of your discussion is what sets the ground work for the important questions at the end of the discussion.

THE ROOM
A Conducive Environment

Most rooms are designed for a specific purpose such as dining, sleeping, or conducting business. You can usually walk into a room and, without being told, ascertain the purpose and the mood of the room by the furniture and its arrangement. In any negotiation or debate type setting, the mood of the room is just as important as the dialogue being presented.

Why do we consider some rooms "formal" and cold while others seem friendly and relaxed even before a word has been said? It is extremely important to keep the mood of the room you are using for a discussion neutral and "open" if you want an interactive dialogue to take place. We need to achieve a perceived balance of power between all people involved and remove the barriers that can cause defensive posturing.

If a room is arranged so that one individual is positioned behind a large, formidable desk with an oversized chair and the other person is ushered to a small chair with no furniture around it, you can be sure the dialogue will be very one sided. Information will be "extracted" and orders will be given instead of ideas and concepts being shared. If intimidation and a one way flow of speech is your goal, this office is perfect for your needs. The only thing missing is a bright light shining in the subject's eyes and cigar smoke blown in their face.

If you plan to have discussions in an office, make sure there is an area that is less formal, and where there are comfortable chairs of similar size. Let it be a more relaxed setting where the visitor will be at ease and willing to "share." If a person is intimidated by their surroundings, they will not be open to participation in any form of dialogue with someone they perceive to be an authority figure.

There is little difference between two people and two teams trying to have an exchange of ideas. Always consider the other group as a single entity. This will help you concentrate on the task before you, and assist in removing the distractions of the multiple personalities across the table from you.

How can we set up a conference room for a proactive state of dialogue? Start by making sure the balance of power appears to be equal. Remove all articles such as banners or flags that are obvious stumbling blocks to open dialogue and defensive attitudes. The chairs should be comfortable and equal in all ways possible for both groups. The lighting should be bright enough for all participants to see, but not glaring. Rooms that are too dark cause emotions to become sullen and subdued. The table should be large enough to provide adequate surface area for the needed papers and related materials. Try to make sure it is not too wide. If a person from one side of the meeting is trying to share papers with an individual from the other team, they must be able to reach across the table without getting to their feet. When a person has to stand up when everyone else around them is sitting, it puts them in a very uncomfortable position. Some individuals will not participate at all if this circumstance occurs. There is little difference between intimidating conversation and inaccessible documents.

Do your best to eliminate distractions. Get rid of the clocks and telephones in the room, and turn off your pagers and cell phones. If the meeting is to be perceived as important, then you need to remove the interruptions within your control. As stated earlier, do not look at your watch if it can be avoided. If the meeting has time restraints, have an individual who is not involved in the negotiations be responsible for informing the group when the meeting is ending.

Make sure there are prearranged breaks in the sessions for human needs. This will help keep the mood of the negotiations from becoming tenser as the stomachs become emptier. It will also give your team time to confer for strategic purposes and allow you to reorganize if necessary. Do not be opposed to having food or drink available during the meeting. This does help keep people in a more open state of mind.

SPECIAL THREAT SITUATIONS

> The Unspoken Dialogue

PACKAGES AND GESTURES

Packages - we see them around us every day. Some large, some small, different colors, different shapes and sizes, from the beginning of our day to the end of our day we see them around us constantly. Often, we try to determine what's in these packages. Could it contain a threat to public safety or some other form of contraband? How can we tell what's inside all of these packages?

It's not the package we need to know about! It's understanding the person who is carrying the package. We can't read minds, but we can read and understand the body gestures of the person who has the package. Reading the gestures of the person carrying the package helps us determine the contents of the package.

Think back for a second - every day you see how people handle things they carry. Think about a supermarket. Think about a person reaching into a cooler area and taking out a container of eggs. How do they handle the eggs? Is it different than how they handle a case of soft drinks? Of course there is a difference. Everyone handles different contents in a different way. We need to look closely at the body gestures of the person handling the contents.

In that same supermarket you will notice a great difference between a person handling a bag of potatoes and a small child. The child will, hopefully, be handled with great caution and care while being placed in and out of the shopping cart seat. Do we think a bag of potatoes will be handled with the same amount of care? This is all human nature. It is the way we all are. You do not have to know the contents of a package to see how the package is being handled. It is the body gestures being displayed by the person who does know what is in the package that are important. How the package is being picked up, carried around, and put down will tell us what is in it.

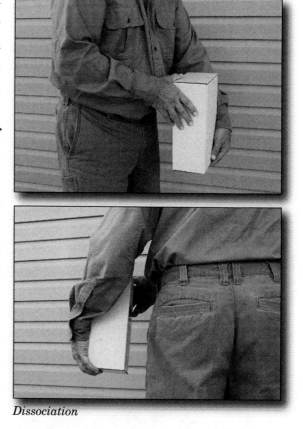

Dissociation

Carrying contraband or carrying something hazardous to public safety will be different than how a person carries routine items or packages. The differences we look for are very clear and very obvious once you know what they are.

A common way contraband is carried is called "dissociation." In other words, they are going to carry the package as if they don't want the package to be part of them. They are not comfortable with it. They're walking and moving with the package uncomfortably away from their body. It's like setting a powerful, spring loaded trap and holding it in the palm of your hand. You wouldn't carry this device close to your body.

Dissociation

You'd carry it out and away from yourself in case it snapped. It's not a bag or a box swinging at your side.

You will also notice that when they put the package down they carefully place it down with a high level of caution. Many times as they set it down they will look at their surroundings and not look at the package. You will see their body posture leaning away from the package. You will also see how they maintain distance away from other people and the package. When people walk near their package they will stand between them and the package or even move the package away from others. If they are in an open area they may stand over the package to guard it. As they are dissociative with the package, they also want others to be physically dissociative with the package.

> The Unspoken Dialogue

Another common way suspicious packages are carried is "parental gestures." This is being literally wrapped around the package. You will observe the body posture curve protectively around the package as if it is a child or small pet. This item is of great importance to them. They aren't just holding it at their side as they walk. They have it up in their arms and are holding it against their chest or stomach, shielding it from the world around them. Whatever they are doing you will notice that they do not relinquish their hold on this package. It constantly remains in their parental type of control. If you are standing near them or approach them, you

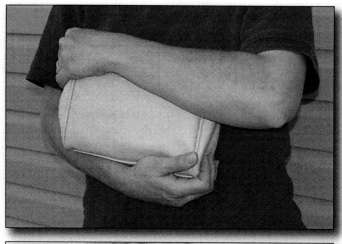

Parental

will notice that they hold the package even tighter and closer. If that package is so important to them then it should also be of great importance to you!

Another type of body gestures an individual with packages can exhibit is "mechanical." With mechanical body gestures the person's appearance is stiff and almost mechanized. They appear to move very deliberately in an almost robotic method. They turn, and then they walk forward. Their movements are stiff and lack flexibility. All of their motion appears to be under total control at all times. The eye gestures are also very robotic. When the head turns left the eyes look left. When the head turns right the eyes look right. The head turns and moves with the movement of the body in a very rigid format. All of the body gestures become literally "locked" together. They will have the appearance of being devoid of emotion and of being more of a transport device than a human being. They will exhibit stiff rigid posture and will walk consistently at one speed. Their voice will be an emotionless monotone.

One very interesting thing about all three types of "carriers" is that before they have the package or after they relinquish control of the package they exhibit normal body signs. Look for the difference. Look for the changes that package causes the person to exhibit.

Remember that body gestures and knowing their meaning is like understanding a language. One body sign is just a few words and a compound gesture becomes a sentence. This means that the more you observe, the more you will understand of this language. The more body signs and gestures you are able to compile, the more accurate your understanding of the person will be.

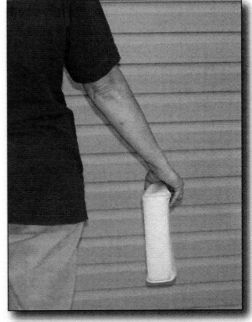

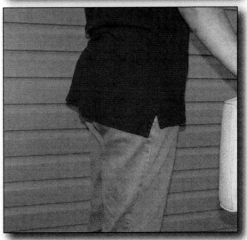

Mechanical

We don't want to draw opinions from a very short story, and we don't want to draw conclusions from only one or two body signs. We want to watch, and gather in as many body signs as possible so that this language breaks down into many paragraphs, which will lead us to a clearer, better, understanding of what we are seeing happening before us.

> The Unspoken Dialogue

APPAREL AND GESTURES

A person can conceal weapons or contraband anywhere on their body. They are not going to tell us verbally where they have put these weapons or contraband but when we watch their body gestures it is a matter of simply "listening" to what they are saying. They tell us through large gestures and some very discrete gestures where the illegal item is. What is a tremendous advantage to us is that they do not even realize that this language exists. All they know is that they have put something in a concealed area and now they are going to continue with their activities without even realizing that their gestures will be giving them away. It is a tremendous advantage to us and it is easy to use against them.

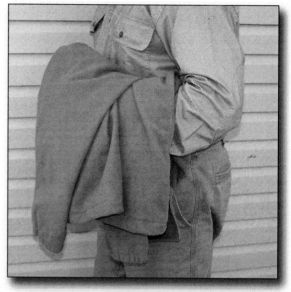

Watch for clothing that is inappropriate for the day or the surrounding conditions. If a person is carrying a heavy overcoat over one arm on a warm day it could be so they can conceal something under the coat. Watch for people wearing raincoats or carrying umbrellas when there are clear skies and no rain predicted. Watch for loose

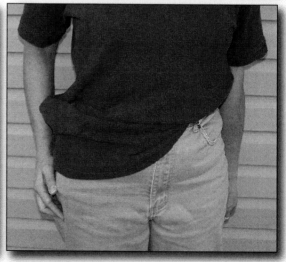

Special Threat Situations

fitting sweaters and vests. Extra layers of clothing allow for more "hiding places". Watch for items of clothing that are being worn unevenly – a shirt that is tucked in on one side but out on the other side to help cover a pocket.

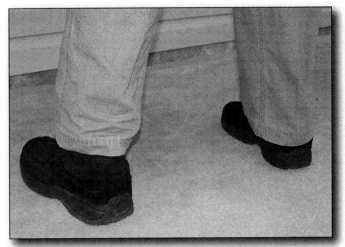

Gravity can help us determine where an individual has hidden contraband on themselves. If they put an item that has any discernable weight in a pocket there will be a noticeable change in the appearance of their apparel. Most individuals that carry a gun illegally are not going to purchase a holster for that gun. They are going to purchase or steal the weapon, and then they are simply going

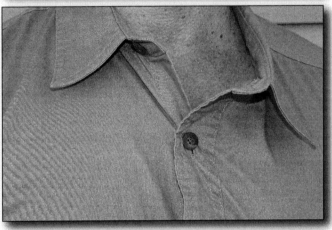

to put it in their pocket. If they are carrying any extra ammunition they will put that into a pocket as well. Don't just check the pockets – check the pant legs. The bottom of the pant leg on the side where the object is will hang down noticeably lower. When a heavy item is in a coat pocket the collar will be pulled down on that side. There can even be a shift or "pulling down" on the side of the jacket if the hidden item has enough weight. Both uneven cuffs and uneven jacket edges are signals for you to look further into the situation.

There is another type of "gravity" that comes into play when you are dealing with people and illegal items. That is the gravity that weighs on the person's mind, their emotions, and sometimes, their guilt. This causes major changes in the person's body gestures. Their hand or arm will stay close or even repeatedly touch the area of concealment to tell us that they are concerned with that pocket or part

> The Unspoken Dialogue

of their apparel. They will cover that area with their arm or hand. They will walk differently; they will move differently. They will swing the arm on the concealed weapon side much less than on the other side causing a very unequal gait in their body movement. A professional will have a means of holding a weapon securely. These individuals will have to be careful that their "contraband" doesn't fall out of its hiding spot.

Just like you can tell when a scale is off balance, with a little bit of practice, you will be able to tell when an individual is "off balance" because they are trying to hide something in their clothing.

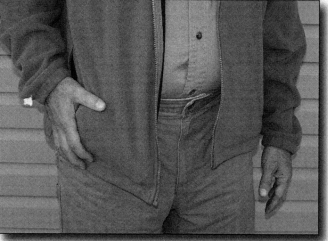

CONCLUSION

CONCLUSION
A Time For Advice

You have been introduced into the incredible world of understanding others at an enhanced level. The pages you have just read are not merely concepts and ideas. They are truly alive in each and every one of us and have been a part of our lives even before we could speak. They remain with us as a viable form of communication even when we become incapacitated or infirmed.

When using these skills, remember to personally display relaxed and neutral body language when dealing with others. Be attentive to what is being said and realize that certain concessions may have to be made in any negotiation scenario. As long as these compromises are not in direct conflict with your position, be it individual or as a group, the requests should be considered. This will help the deliberations from becoming stagnant and avoid having the conversation becoming one sided.

In order to successfully manipulate dialogue, we need to be able to instill in others the perspectives and objectives that are important to our position. We need to remember what causes negative posturing from the opposition and avoid or eliminate further gestures that can create a defensive position.

Bear in mind that the skills you have learned need to be practiced and developed. Just as a child takes many practice steps before he or she can run, it will take time for you to perceive all *The Unspoken Dialogue* that is around us every day.

AFTERWORDS

> The Unspoken Dialogue

Comments of William L. Budd, Ph.D.

After a 25 year career as a police officer, Robert Rail, consumed by the desire to learn and experience more, became an international police officer in 1999, and served one year in the United Nations Mission in Bosnia-Herzegovina. Unlike his law enforcement experiences in the United States, he saw a vastly different set of circumstances. The effects of a long civil conflict, followed by an international war in Yugoslavia presented Bob with a large and complex field laboratory. Driven by his insatiable desire to learn and experience, Bob undertook a study of people who had suffered under tyranny, oppression, deprivation, stress, fear, indignation, persecution, displacement, injury, torture, and the horrors of death. The product of his pioneering work was *The Unspoken Dialogue*, first published in 2001.

I met Bob in September 2002 when we were both in training for deployment to the United Nation Mission in Kosovo. There was little time then for long introductions and comparisons of experience - that would happen later - but I was already aware of his previous mission work. After training, I was fortunate to be teamed with Bob and we were deployed into the very heart of what had been the Serbian/Kosovar civil war in the 1990's. There we were, two American officers amid a sea of hatred, violence, aggression, religious, political, and international conflict.

Working closely with Bob was an opportunity I had never expected. Although I knew he was veteran international police officer, it was during our assignment together that I came to appreciate and benefit from his experiences. Working with Bob - sharing the same residence, and surviving in an extremely hostile environment for 27 months - was an incredible experience. Although I had a significant career in law enforcement and had attended training programs including interview techniques, body language, martial arts and many, many more, none were comparable in the quality and depth of knowledge that Bob presented in *"The Unspoken Dialogue."*

Because we had different backgrounds, Bob and I were eventually redeployed to different assignments, but continued what had become a well established working partnership. Bob was assigned to the UN Mission Police Training Center, Pristina, Kosovo, to serve as the senior Selection Assessment Testing officer. I went on to serve as the Officer In Charge of the Kosovo Police Professional Standards Unit. In my new position I suddenly found a greater than ever expected need for very specialized interview, negotiations and understanding of "body signs."

The working environment in Pristina was vastly different from that in the USA, and required finely tuned expertise in order to effectively deal with not only the Kosovars, but an international staff from more than 50 other countries. Life in a UN mission is very different from work in the USA. Local customs, cultural, societal, religious, political, and language variations poses a great threat; anyone who has ever served in a foreign mission will recognized this as an understatement. To survive and succeed, it was crucial that we call into action all of the skills at our disposal. Again, Bob's research, writing, and experience proved its worth each and every day.

Some months later I was assigned to serve as the Senior Planner for the UN's Transition program and then appointed Director of Transition. The myriad duties of that post included intense field negotiations with Albanian, Serbian, Bosnian, Turkish, Greek, and many other groups. As the American charged with getting the Transition program on track, I had literally hundreds of high level meetings with disparate groups. Not all of those meetings were pleasant, but all were successful. While I relied heavily upon my well established communication, negotiation, and interview skills, it was the *"body language"* skills I learned from Bob that gave me a critical advantage to prevail and succeed with landmark achievements.

Looking back on this incredible experience I can't help but wonder how much better I could have performed in any of my many other previous positions in law enforcement, military reserve, family life, politics, and even as a university professor if I had been able to apply Bob Rail's body language skills. Such knowledge would have most assuredly provided me with an incredible advantage. This new edition of *The Unspoken Dialogue* with updated information, photos, and anecdotes should be considered a "tool" of one's trade and, if applied, is sure to maximize the best outcomes possible. It is evident that thousands of people around the globe have benefited from Bob's work and, although I cannot speak for them, I am certain they too, are indelibly transformed.

William L. Budd, Ph.D.
Professor, Lynn University and Jones College, Florida

> The Unspoken Dialogue

Comments of Jeffrey P. Rush, DPA

Robert Rail's 25 years of experience as a Chicagoland copper informs all as to what he is and does, but perhaps no more so than in the words of this book. His years of law enforcement service have led him to understand that it is more than just what people say that's important, but it is how they act, what they do, and what their body tells us that is equally as important, and in many cases substantially more important.

In no other line of work is this understanding more important than in the warrior professions. Sure, it would be nice to know if the person sitting on the barstool next to you is "interested" in you, but knowing or not knowing that will not kill you. But not understanding the body language of the person standing in front of you at a ticket counter or walking beside you in the mall might put you at risk. If you're a cop, and you can't read the body language of the driver you just pulled over, or the guy who decided to pull a "stop and rob" at a convenience store, then that could very easily result in yours or someone else's leath.

Moms everywhere know whether or not their child is lying or upset or even in trouble and, more often than not, this understanding is not based on what the child says, but how they act. When I was young I got a traffic ticket. It wasn't a major crime but I was seriously worried about what my parents would say. It was a rule at our house that, regardless of the time, I was required to tell my parents that I was home. The night I got the ticket, I stood in the doorway of their bedroom and announced that I was home. My Mother, waking from a deep sleep immediately asked, "What's wrong?" My reply was, "Nothing." She shot up in bed and said, "I know better than that, what is it?" I told her. Years later I asked her how she knew something was wrong, and she told me that it was something about how I was "acting." A number of signs that I unknowingly exhibited just "said to her" that something was wrong. People everywhere exhibit involuntary signs and this is but one of the reasons that *The Unspoken Dialogue* is such an important book.

In this time of global danger and uncertainty it is important to know that body language is universal; it is evident in both sexes and all races and cultures. In other words, it is not just in the United States where one's body "talks," the body speaks regardless of where it comes from. Robert Rail's service in Kosovo as a warrior-trainer is evidence of the universal language of the body and lends even more credibility and importance to his work and book.

It has been reported that when Mohammed Atta, one of the 9/11 hijackers, approached the airport ticket counter that infamous day, the airline clerk just "felt like something was wrong." He could not put his finger on it, but the way Atta was acting made him uncomfortable. It wasn't anything that Atta *said* that got the clerk's attention, but his body was communicating. The clerk said nothing to anyone for fear of being accused of racial profiling or worse.

My life partner is the Security Director at an upscale shopping mall. She has developed a keen understanding that it is oftentimes how people act, not what they are saying, that provides substantive information. She has caught many a thief, and recovered thousands of dollars in merchandise based initially on what the bad guy's body was "telling" her. Indeed, in assisting Loss Prevention officers of various stores, on many occasions she has focused on the suspect's "unspoken dialogue" while the LP officer focused on the words being spoken. She has gleaned substantially more information reading body language than the LP did just listening to words.

She and I also work special events, concerts, and executive protection security. Sometimes the noise level at these events makes it hard to hear what people are saying, it is extremely important to be able to read a person's body language. Is that person in the front row about to jump on stage? Is the guy at the Hank Williams, Jr. show about to pour beer on the guy in front of him? Is this person coming up to the gate trying to hide something – maybe booze, a knife, a gun? These are all questions that we must answer and in some cases respond to. I cannot count the number of times after responding that we are asked, "How did you know?" We knew because the unspoken dialogue told us.

Knowing and understanding the importance of the unspoken dialogue is critical when providing executive protection. As you scan the crowd for potential "hostiles" you have only the unspoken dialogue to go on. Is that person about to pull a gun, throw something, or attack the principal? You need to answer those questions immediately so that you can go into action. You generally don't have the opportunity to ask the suspect, "Are you about to pull a gun?" And even if you could, they would probably lie. You must make decisions based on the unspoken dialogue, and more often than not, your decision is the right one.

I know that the voice is the window to the subject's intentions. I also know that there are various signs and signals that sometimes agree with the voice and sometimes do not. When the voice and signs disagree, we believe the body language. So too does Bob Rail.

> The Unspoken Dialogue

Rudy Giuliani, "America's Mayor," believes that suicide bombing is the worst threat we face. Henry Morgenstern, of Security Solutions International, suggests that one of the points in the process where suicide bombers can be stopped is as they approach the target. Whether approaching, or getting their nerve up, or just waiting for the "right moment," the point is that the only way to identify them will be by how they are acting, their unspoken dialogue. We must therefore, be aware of what the body says and how to interpret it. There are numerous examples of lives saved, merchandise recovered, and life made better for everyone because someone was able to interpret body language.

That is the importance of *The Unspoken Dialogue* – it helps save lives. Robert Rail, in this easy to read yet comprehensive book walks you through how to read and understand the unspoken dialogue. He explains how the body just can't lie about some things, and how the body just can't help but telegraph some movement, e.g., if someone is in a chair, they can't get up without first leaning forward. Bob, in a clear and concise way provides both the theory behind *The Unspoken Dialogue* and the specific tactics and techniques needed to understand and apply it. He does this in a clear, concise, simple, and straight forward manner.

It should also be noted that *The Unspoken Dialogue* has been translated into several languages, and is required reading in many European and African police academies. So too, it should be required reading in American police academies. *The Unspoken Dialogue* is, without question, one of the books that should be on the bookshelf of every "warrior" and should be one of the most referenced tools in their repertoire. It is one of maybe half a dozen books that will save your life! Read it, absorb it, live it, and share it with your colleagues and peers throughout the world. It is that good.

One last suggestion, should you ever have the opportunity, as I have, to attend one of Bob's training sessions, do so. You will come away a substantially better trained individual than when you went in. Too much of the training we endure is simply not applicable or that good. I can attest to the fact that training by Robert Rail does not fall into that category, it is simply that good.

Jeffrey P. Rush, DPA
Assistant Professor of Criminal Justice
The University of Louisiana at Monroe

About the Author

Dr. Robert R. Rail is recognized internationally as one of the foremost experts on managing interpersonal relations. He has taught his "understanding body language" techniques and methods to people from more than 60 countries.

As a consultant to the United Nations in the Balkans and Iraq, Dr. Rail was responsible for designing curriculum and instructing elite police officers from 56 nations who have been deployed in Bosnia, Kosovo, Iraq, Jordan, Asia, and Africa. He was also named as a physical confrontation advisor and resource training provider to select personnel of NATO and OSCE (Organization for Security & Co-Operation in Europe).

Dr. Rail was a resident instructor at the Specialized Advanced Training Unit of the High Institute of Baghdad Police College, and was awarded a second doctorate degree for his exceptional abilities as an international instructor. He has received numerous other awards for his work in the international community.

Dr. Rail has an outstanding background of over a quarter of a century of both martial arts knowledge and "on the street" law enforcement experience. He is an internationally respected and acclaimed master instructor. Through all his classes, lectures, presentations and even casual contacts, he displays a constant flow of encouragement, enthusiasm, and instructional humor.

Dr. Rail is a frequent contributor to television and radio programs, and periodicals. He conducts both training and consulting services for universities and corporations worldwide.

He is the author of four books: *The Unspoken Dialogue; Defense Without Damage; Custodial Cuffing & Restraint;* and *Reactive Handcuffing Tactics.*